Front cover: *Hapet Perfect,*
a yellow/lavender blend

The Herbert Brown Class at
the National Show, a class
where individual Dahlia
Societies' members can
contribute blooms towards
an overall exhibit.

DAHLIAS FOR YOU

TED COLLINS

A NATIONAL DAHLIA SOCIETY PUBLICATION

DAHLIAS FOR YOU
A National Dahlia Society Publication
First published 2010

Written by Ted Collins,
President of the National Dahlia Society

Edited by the National Dahlia Society
Publications Committee

Design and layout by Carol Seatory

Photographs individually attributed

Printed by Lancing Press

For up-to-date National Dahlia Society
information visit: www.dahlia-nds.co.uk

ISBN 978-0-904074-01-7

CONTENTS

INTRODUCTION

Dahlias have never been as popular as they are now in the 21st Century, providing the gardener with a wealth of colour, over an extended period and for a variety of uses.

Ted Collins, President of the National Dahlia Society

They are easy to grow, once a few basic details are mastered and they will then provide an abundance of bloom from year to year and the bounty of new fresh tubers for use the following year.

This book offers an insight into the basic details whilst whetting the reader's appetite to grow this wonderful flower. We intend, by the provision of best quality photographs with appropriate text, to enable you the reader to get the best from the dahlia. We also illustrate the best of the current dahlias. Included in it is what to do and when to do it, also where to go to see dahlias at their best.

What is a dahlia? It is a member of the compositae group of plants that includes asters, helianthus, chrysanthemums and several thousand other species.

Found originally on the semi-tropical slopes in Mexico it is, however, a fairly adaptable plant and has been bred worldwide, over the years, by hybridists and amateurs alike.

In the UK trials, exhibitions and gardens utilising the best of modern dahlias are open to visitors. This is also a common practice in the USA, Australia, New Zealand, Holland and other European countries.

Photograph page 4:
An arrangement of dahlias showing the vast range

In each country certain dahlias perform better than perhaps in another country, so some cultivars are more popular than others. Occasionally a cultivar will perform well in many countries.

In the Northern hemisphere they flower between June and November, whilst in the Southern hemisphere, it is between January and May.

The range of size is amazing, from the tiny single blooms to the fully double; spectacular giant-size blooms are grown throughout the world and are mostly raised by keen amateur specialists.

The shape can vary from star, anemone, collerette, paeony, decorative, ball, pompon, cactus, fimbriated, orchid, waterlily and miscellaneous types. All forms and their uses are covered in this publication.

The National Dahlia Society stand at Malvern Show which highlights many of the dahlia forms

Regarding colour, any of the these dahlias can be either white, various shades of yellow, orange, bronze, flame, red, pink, lilac, lavender, mauve, purple, wine, or violet. They may be combined in blends, bi-colours, or variegations. We await in anticipation a blue dahlia!

A spectacular arrangement of collerettes staged in bowls

You can see from this that the possibilities are endless for growing dahlias. So do not be surprised that there are types, not usually grown by gardeners and which are not mentioned above, such as the tree dahlia or *Dahlia Tenuicaulis*, which would normally grow to about nine metres high, although they can be pruned to remain only about a metre high.

**Ted Collins, President of
the National Dahlia Society**

Dahlias used in a bed mixed with perrenials and annuals, at Hilary Barnes' award-winning garden in Sussex

HISTORY

As we tell the story of the dahlia through this book we take time here to give you just a few notes on its origins and how the dahlia arrived into the modern world.

Dahlias originated on the semi-tropical mountainous slopes of Mexico. The Aztecs grew dahlias, not the types we know, but tree dahlias which grew to heights of between ten and fourteen feet high.

The blooms, by modern standards, were fairly nondescript red and mauve single blooms. The Aztecs, it is believed, used the hollow stems for irrigation purposes and the blooms as part of their religious rituals.

The Conquistadors from Spain discovered the dahlia in the mid seventeenth century and research was carried out, funded by the then king of Spain into various aspects of Aztec life. The dahlia was known to the Aztecs as "acocotli" or "hollow pipe" and became better known to Spain.

It was in Spain at the end of the eighteenth century that the dahlia first arrived in Europe. Seed was sent from Mexico to the Madrid Botanical Gardens, which eventually found its way to the Abbe Cavanniles, who was a botanist at the botanical gardens. These seeds were of a new species and the most eminent botanist then was Linneas. He declined the opportunity to give his name to the new plant material, so the honour fell to Andres Dahl, the leading Swedish botanist. Such is fate, so no Linneas shows for the "acocotli".

Some seed found its way to England as well as to other European countries. At that time, however, the needs for propagating meant only a rich man could afford to grow dahlias. Plants changed hands at what were then equivalent of the average yearly wage. The dahlia, like the pineapple, became a symbol of social status. The blooms grown then were eventually classified as peonies, that is: single decoratives.

Hapet Ideal, a colourful semi-cactus dahlia

Eventually, in the early nineteenth century with the industrial revolution, people became more affluent and leisure activities increased, including access to and participation in growing specialist cultivars.

In the first half of the nineteenth century, horticultural societies were formed and shows held.

In Germany, botanists changed the name dahlia to Georgina, to honour a Russian botanist, but this name soon went out of worldly fashion.

However, in Germany, pompon dahlias were created. In England botanists produced the forerunner of the ball dahlia when show and fancy types appeared. Not to be left out, France produced the collerettes.

So, towards the end of the nineteenth century, most of our modern dahlias had arrived. The last to appear came again from Mexico in a collection of

A bowl of single dahlias shown for effect

unnamed tubers sent to Holland. One of these produced yellow blooms with thin, spiky petals. It was named Juarez, after the then President of Mexico. It was the cultivar from which all modern cactus dahlias derived. The march of the modern dahlia had begun.

FURTHER READING

Dahlias a Colour Guide by Ted Collins published by Crowood, ISBN 1-86126-582-4

A Gardener's Guide to Growing Dahlias by Gareth Rowlands, published by David & Charles, ISBN 0-7153-0858-0

Dahlias by Ted Collins published by New Plant Library, ISBN 0-7548-0499-4

Encyclopaedia of Dahlias by Bill McClaren published by Timber Press, ISBN 0-88192-658-2

SO WHERE DO YOU START?

Wherever you live, you should first find the nearest place to you where dahlias are grown. It may be on an allotment or it may be in a garden of a house where you see dahlias growing. If you really want to know more, call at that allotment when someone is there, or at the house, and ask about the dahlias. Provided you do it at a reasonable time, any real dahlia grower will respond.

North West Cosmos, single dahlia

Check local information sources for details of local horticultural societies and go to one of their meetings and check out their schedule of shows and events. If there are dahlias on the menu, join that society and seek out the dahlia fans.

Go on to the internet, type in 'dahlias' and a whole new world will open up for you. You will find, amongst a plethora of sites, that of the National Dahlia Society and your knowledge base will start to grow. If you are not computer literate, buy gardening magazines and you will find details of the National Dahlia Society.

Amongst all this wealth of information will be advertisements for a number of dahlia nurseries or dahlia suppliers. Many of these now have pictures of dahlia cultivars that they have on sale on their web site. Some are in the UK, others in the countries mentioned before, many of whom export tubers. Also, there will be details of other dahlia societies, possibly within reasonable travelling distance, most of which hold plant sales for tubers and rooted cuttings, to raise funds to support that society.

From the pictures seen on the web site, make a note of the ones that appeal to you. Some words of caution here before you place your order. It is said that pictures do not lie but sometimes, unintentionally, they can mislead. Try to see what you want, when it is in bloom, before you buy.

More importantly how much can you afford, not only financially but in the amount of time you can give to growing them to perfection? If you want them just for garden display what time do you give now?

If you get hooked on exhibiting, then as a yard-stick think in terms of one hour of work per hundred plants per day from July to October. Get your plan set out early and stick to it throughout the season. There will be many temptations in the future as your knowledge and experience grows.

Moonfire, a particularly pretty dwarf bedding dahlia with dark foliage

HOW TO BEGIN

Dahlias are long established as garden and or exhibition plants. Some dahlia fans will tell you that if the dahlia only had scent, no other species would be grown because of the dahlia range of form and colour. They can be grown from seed, cuttings or tubers, the choice is yours.

What do you want from this flexible flower?
- A riot of colour in your garden throughout the summer and autumn?
- Cut flowers for display at home, in your office or place of worship?
- Competition at local, area or national flower shows?

Any or all of these can be yours. First, consult your plan and ask yourself again how much time you can spend with the plants and what space is available within easy reach of where you are based. This book will help you: firstly to answer the questions above and then to help you achieve the best results for whatever use you intend for the dahlias of your choice; starting with the basics then the various methods to ensure success, whatever your choice.

Pooh, an unusual collerette

A display of single orchid (star) dahlias

A basket display of dahlia *Nepos*, a small waterlily

Twynings' After Eight

Honka

Patio types:
Jewel Orange
Jewel Purple
Jewel Salmon
Jewel White

IN YOUR GARDEN

Dahlias can be grown for:
- Border display
- Patio containers
- Perennial display
- Conservatory use.

Summer bedding is what a lot of gardeners grow for border use. They can be geraniums, impatiens, begonias and salvias amongst other types.

The dahlia can be used to great effect as summer bedding. This can be achieved by either utilising large blocks of a single variety which can be a self-colour or mixed colour. Alternatively, they can be planted in mixed cultivars toward the backs of beds containing other summer bedding.

In the border, the dahlia can be effective in withstanding extremes of weather and require less water, once established, than most other bedding plants.

All they require is the removal of dead heads to continue flowering, from late June until frosts in November.

Block planting with various colour dahlias in box hedging, at the Chateau Villandry

There are a number of types that excel for bedding use: lilliput, gallery and dwarf cultivars, which usually grow between 25 and 75 cm in height, also miniature cactus or decorative types which grow to a height between 75 and 105 cm. They produce large volumes of bloom throughout the season when planted in the garden border, at about 30 cm (one foot) apart.

The National Dahlia Society Classified Directory (updated every two years) lists cultivars to use in your garden.

Examples are:
- **Lilliput**: *Amanda* (pink), *Brownie* (orange), *Exotic Dwarf* (pink)
- **Gallery:** *Art Deco* (orange), *Degas* (pink), *Rembrandt* (pink & white)
- **Dwarf:** *Jewel Pink, Jewel Orange, Jewel Salmon*
- **Dark Leaf Varieties:** *Bishop of Llandaff* (red), *Moonfire* (yellow), *David Howard* (orange bronze), *Fire Mountain* (red), *Swanlake* (white)
- **Miniature Cactus:** *Glenbunk Twinkle* (white/red), *So Dainty* (bronze), *Weston Pirate* (red), *Weston Spanish Dancer* (red/yellow)
- **Miniature Decoratives:** *Barbarry Banker* (pink), *Doris Duke* (red).

PATIO USE

New homes, as well as some town houses, do not have large gardens. Many will only have a patio, for barbecues and similar social functions where during warm summer days a small glass of one's favourite beverage can be enjoyed.

This is where the dahlia can score. A riot of colour can be provided by the correct choice of dahlia. These can be planted and grown in pots or containers of all sizes, or in beds which may be provided in decking or paving.

Good drainage and a friable soil are basic requirements for the plants. One advantage of this method of growth is that no support is required during the season and apart from watering and dead heading, no other work is required. Although planting in small beds or pots will require more daily watering than with other growing methods. More frequent application of a soluble fertiliser will also be necessary to obtain the best results. Twice-weekly feeds will greatly improve the amount and colour of the blooms on the plant.

The de-heading of spent blooms will, again, ensure a season long provision of flower.

Flowering will continue until the first frost of the winter. All dahlias are susceptible to, and are blackened by, frost when the water contained in the stems freezes and destroys the tissue. When frost is forecast, the containers of dahlias can be removed and stored in a frost-free place.

Cultivars to use

Once again, gallery dahlias are recommended. In addition to those already mentioned for garden use, other cultivars are: *Art Nouveau* (pink/purple), *Cezanne* (yellow), *Renoir* (pink). Lilliput cultivars recommended in addition to those for garden use are: *Omo* (white), *Little Dorrit* (purple), *Lilliput Orange* (orange). Also Jewel types, *Petite Harvest* (gold), *Petite Sunrise* (yellow).

PERENNIAL DISPLAY

Dahlias come into their own in bedding displays. Dark foliage type dahlias can be used to create a focal or hot spot in a bed, by using one or perhaps three plants in the midst of impatiens or begonias or similar bedding material.

The earliest modern dark foliaged cultivar was the red paeony flowered dahlia, *Bishop of Llandaff*, raised

Marie Schnugg, a star dahlia

in 1928 but still a wow factor in many gardens. There are many newer dark-foliaged dahlias that can be used, such as *David Howard*, an orange/bronze blended miniature decorative raised in 1965, *Moonfire*, a dwarf orange blended single raised in 1991 and *Fire Mountain*, a miniature red decorative raised in 1999. A taller variety is *Twynings' After Eight*, a single white variety raised in 2004.

If you want something different, why not try *Mexican Black* in your border.It has a smell of dark chocolate, being a dahlia/cosmos cross.

In addition to the above, *Dahlia X Hortensis* or other species such as *Dahlia Imperialis* or *Dahlia Tenuicaulis* can be used, but only really when you have gained experience with the garden varieties.

Once again, plan carefully choosing height and colour that will fit with whatever bedding plants you will also use.

CONSERVATORY

For those who want something different in their conservatory, tree dahlias are a must. Tree dahlias, *Dahlia Tenuicaulis*, and its hybrids, left to their own devices, will grow as in the wild to nine metres or more. This is probably too high for most domestic conservatories.

However, pruned regularly, they will grow well at one to two metres providing brilliant copper foliage flowering with single blooms in October and November depending on growing conditions.

YOUR WINDOW BOX

Dahlias are so adaptable. No room in your border or your patio? Still wanting to grow dahlias? No problem if you have room for window boxes.

Star dahlias are available, growing to a height of 25 to 35 centimetres, in a variety of colours, with all the characteristics of the larger brothers and sisters in the species.

In good, well-drained soil, well watered and fed during the summer and autumn and dead headed from time to time they will give a riot of colour. Just under your window, they will wow you and your neighbours too.

Cultivars to choose from are the Jewel range, which have a petite growing habit and a wide range of colours. Other dwarf growers are the Topmix range which include: *Omo* (white), *Exotic Dwarf* (pink), and *Little Dorrit* (purple). *Hy Scent* (red/yellow) as its name suggests has a slight fragrance, use near your bedroom window.

DAHLIA USE IN FLOWER ARRANGEMENTS

Dahlias can be used to great effect in baskets or bowls or even in a pedestal arrangement for your home, office or church. The containers can come in all shapes and sizes, from conventional round to oblong or square or cornucopia shape both large and small. All containers must have an impervious base or saucer-type container in the bottom to hold the water and perhaps a layer of plastic underneath, as the dahlias will not survive long out of water.

Sometimes a block of oasis will be fastened, sitting in the base which is then thoroughly soaked. The dahlia stalks are then carefully arranged, as any floral artist will tell you, with the stalks cut at varying lengths so that each bloom in the basket or bowl, can be seen to best advantage. Ideally, the blooms in the back row should just touch or be below a handle if the basket has a handle. If different-sized blooms are used then the larger ones should ideally be in the centre.

Where do you get the blooms from? Well, in this instance the plants would have to be grown in your garden somewhere, if not in the border then a special nursery bed, or they can be obtained from specialist growers.

The smaller cultivars are best as they will frame and add colour to any arrangement to great effect. Varieties to be grown are very similar to your window box types but in addition *Lorona Dawn* (pink/white), *Sophie Taylor* (orange/yellow), *North Star* (white), *Hy Scent* (red yellow) and *Honka Surprise* (red/yellow); older varieties such as *Honka* (yellow) and *Marie Schnugg* (red).

YOUR CHOICE – WHAT GRABS YOU

Having produced a plan, having visited places where dahlias are grown locally and elsewhere, having checked your diary and the space where you hope to grow dahlias you now have to make choices.

- Are you going to grow for the garden or exhibition?
- Have you had your soil analysed? Should you?

Dahlias thrive best if the soil is on the acid side of neutral that is about 6.5 pH. It is not essential, but if in doubt get your soil tested, either professionally or do it yourself with a soil testing kit.

Whatever you do, it is important that the soil is well drained. Dahlias are water greedy but must not be waterlogged. Their thin early roots can stretch to a metre and get fatter nearer the crown or centre of the plant and these fatter roots become the tubers storing starter food for next year's plants.

It is a good idea, if weather and other duties permit, to get the dahlia patch dug over before winter frosts really set in. Frosts will break up the soil far you better than you can.

Dahlias, except pompons, really thrive on soil that has organic fertiliser applied from time to time, perhaps in alternative years depending how good your soil was when you started. This may be dug in during springtime, or it may be applied as mulch when the dahlias are planted.

A word of caution: many growers have had disaster strike, using animal manure and the like. The animal owner has fed the animal with feed containing herbicides, or has treated its pasture with herbicide. The animals are immune but the dahlia is not.

Nothing is worse than planting out good plants and then seeing them looking gnarled and deformed. Before buying, ask your source if there is a possibility that the animal feed has included herbicide.

The alternative is to make your own compost. Many local authorities also compost garden waste. They should and usually do use heat treatment to get the end result. However, there is a danger that in home-grown compost, unless the compost heap gets up to a really good temperature, you may simply recycle last year's diseases from last year's dahlia foliage or other infected garden waste

In addition to organic feed, inorganic fertilisers can be useful. Fish, blood and bone mixtures are excellent as are similar proprietary brands like Growmore. Use according to the suppliers' recommendations and spread and hoe in prior to planting.

Next to be considered is planting out. How you do it may well be governed by how you intend preventing moisture evaporation from the ground. Dahlias really appreciate mulching – that is covering the ground around the plants with a moisture-retaining material. This could be woven plastic matting which can be purchased in rolls a metre wide, in varying thickness gauges. It is usually black and fixing pegs can be bought separately. Whilst retaining moisture in the ground, being of a woven material, it permits water from above to permeate through.

If this is your choice, then spread the roll out across the area you intend to grow your dahlias and make a cross shaped cut in the material where required for the insertion of the plant into the ground. When cutting out the holes for exhibition purposes, allow at least 45 cm between pompons, 60 cm between small and miniature varieties, 70 cm at least for medium varieties and 90 cm for large and giant varieties.

Before fixing the matting in order to combat slugs, spread pellets of Metaldehyde on the ground, or water in a solution of the same, but be careful this chemical is harmful to humans, animals and birds and lethal to slugs and snails.

This matting serves a dual purpose as it not only retains moisture in the ground, reducing the need for watering, it also prevents weeds from growing around the dahlia plants.

Another alternative is straw which is much cheaper than plastic, but again a risk can be taken as it may have been sprayed with herbicides, it is also a good home for pests such as slugs, earwigs and or red spider.

It should be placed around the plants after planting out, usually after rain. Take care to allow a space around the plant stem say two or three inches in diameter, to prevent stem rot. Straw certainly retains the moisture in the ground but in very hot dry weather it is at risk of catching fire, especially if smokers are around or you decide on a bonfire near by during the growing season.

A further alternative is mushroom compost, preferably inert, or you may end up with an unexpected mushroom farm on your patch or your neighbours. Similarly, spread it around the plants when planted out and keep away from the plant stem. The growing media for mushrooms contains chemicals so you need to test the soil after using mushroom compost. It is best left to weather for at least a year on a heap.

The start of good cultivation is not over yet.

Before planting out another decision is required. Dahlias during the height of the growing season can become quite big plants. Equally certain is that just at the wrong time there will be summer rain, heavy rain, possibly a storm.

Expect that some of the time there will be strong winds. How will you provide support for the plants? There is no doubt that the taller growing cultivars need support.

Plant showing the three cane method of support

Traditionally, three canes or stakes have been placed in a triangle equally distant from each other around the plant, These then have twine or a similar material wound round the canes or stakes one lower and one higher from the ground, with the diameter and height of the canes or stakes depending on the height of the plant and type of the variety chosen.

It is useful when purchasing dahlia cultivars, to find out from the dahlia supplier the usual height of the variety and to grow varieties of roughly the same height near to each other. This is particularly true if you decide to support your dahlia plants with weld mesh or similar. Weld mesh is basically a roll of material, composed usually of galvanised wire or plastic squares 10 cm or 15 cm in size.

(Additionally, if you are thinking of exhibiting for large and giant varieties, some form of covering or shading is essential. Find out from the supplier or a local exhibitor and the answers may persuade you to grow these varieties also near each other.)

The weld mesh is spread out on the planting bed, then the plants are then put in the ground, each in the appropriate square using the recommended planting distances mentioned earlier. Soon after, the mesh is carefully lifted and fixed to a single cane or stake of each plant, at about twelve inches above soil level and at the requisite distance apart of your

25

How to support with mesh,
also showing the drip line

Close-up of the mesh

planting out plan. There may be only one layer of mesh used, or perhaps later another layer will be needed on top at a higher level.

As the plants grow the mesh is raised to ensure that when necessary the plants will be supported. So starting at about a foot off the ground the mesh will be raised in stages to perhaps three feet off the ground, keeping the body of the plant within the mesh.

Care must be taken in raising it, but even with the greatest care taken there will be some loss of leaf and or branch, just try not to lose too much.

So you have sorted out the soil, decided on the mulch to be provided, the plants planted and now it is time to relax and do other gardening jobs, or go on holiday.

Leave your dahlias to settle in, but ensure that they are not nipped in the bud by slugs or snails. So, before taking that well-earned rest, make sure you have taken precautions accordingly by spreading pellets or watering in metaldehyde if you have not done so already. As someone has said before, slugs will leave lettuce and tender garden plants and they will gather in your dahlias. One grower even suggested that you throw your slug pellets over next door's fence to draw them away from your dahlias!

PROPAGATION

So far this book has concentrated on the reader starting to grow dahlias having bought or been given plants or tubers to plant out and grow. Eventually, once you have started growing dahlias, you will want to produce your own plants. Once you do, you will have entered another fascinating part of the dahlia world.

The dahlia is very bountiful not only in blooms but in its ease of propagation. The simplest way to multiply your plants is by splitting a clump of tubers.

Be bold and take a sharp spade or knife with the tubers on a hard surface. You must do this when the "eyes" or new buds are just showing on the "crown" of the tubers which is usually some time in March. The "crown" is where the tuber meets the main stem. To produce a new plant you must have an "eye" and at least one tuber together.

In the USA this is how many dahlias are sold and they are called "chicken legs". The "chicken legs" can be planted in a pot or straight into the ground as this combination of "eye" and tuber will produce next year a plant and tubers just as if you used old tubers or new plants.

It is best, of course, to give some time to your new "plant" by acclimatising it to the outside temperature before planting out, by placing it in a cold frame.

Many enthusiasts of dahlia propagation think a greenhouse is essential. It is desirable but not necessarily essential. The benefits of the warmth of a greenhouse can be partially achieved by purchasing or making your own garden frame.

This need not be costly or elaborate. I can report one being made from materials rescued from the demolition of our local police station. Officially, that is, it was being rebuilt – not the result of local villains' activities.

No-one, except this impoverished dahlia grower wanted the windows, roof members or floor boards. So, for a few pence for wood screws, a two metre by one metre garden frame was duly constructed. Eventually, an electric tubular heater was installed and the frame's use extended. With a heated greenhouse or frame, almost any type of propagation of dahlias is possible.

Ideally, first set up tubers in February, that is either direct on the bench or in trays, then put your dahlias in a growing medium, which can be peat or potting compost, remembering that the tubers already contain enough supply of nutrients to start them growing.

Tubers set up in boxes

The crown should be just above the top of the growing medium as it is important that this area does not rot or suffer mildew. To avoid this happening, some crowns with a hollow stem, need preparation before setting up, or plunging. This usually takes the form of drilling out the middle of the main stem as well as removing damaged tubers.

29

Sulphur powder can also protect against mildew, liberally applied to the stump of the stem before plunging.

If your clump is too big, remove whole tubers rather than cutting them in half, as the feeding hairs normally start to grow from the end of the tuber.

Dahlias respond to warmth from below and moisture from above and make sure the growing media used is well drained, and do not over water, until they start into growth. Use warm water in the early stages not cold water direct from a hose. Dahlias at no stage enjoy waterlogged conditions.

They will grow in temperatures anywhere from 10 degrees centigrade to 20 degrees centigrade, growing quicker the higher the temperature and liking fairly humid conditions.

Depending on the conditions in the greenhouse, buds will start to show in two weeks or so from start up. Once the buds get going there will soon be shoots with leaves. You then need to consider the taking of cuttings.

CUTTINGS

There are two methods of taking cuttings.

The most commonly used method is when the shoot on the crown has two pair of leaves; a sharp blade is used to detach the shoot from the crown of the tuber.

The cut must leave sufficient of the original "eye" left on the crown to ensure further shoots will grow from this original "eye". Dormant eyes will then form and make more shoots. Within another ten days or so, further shoots will appear on the crown enabling further cuttings to be taken.

Growth eyes appearing

The ends of the cutting taken should be further trimmed if necessary just below the original leaf joint. The cutting is then usually dipped in a hormone powder or hormone liquid to encourage root growth. Make sure that the rooting powder is freshly purchased as it deteriorates with keeping. Some growers can propagate without rooting powder and certainly in April, cuttings will readily root without this stimulus. The cutting should then be placed in a rooting medium.

Almost any compost will do, if well-drained, usually however a self made mixture of one part sharp sand to one part peat. If compost is purchased instead of peat it is still useful to mix sand at the same rate, this will keep the compost "open".

The rooting mixture can be contained in virtually any type of container made of any kind of material.

Many years ago clay pots were most often recommended and used, with the cuttings inserted around the rim. Nowadays plastic multi-cell trays are more often used to contain the rooting compost. The advantage these containers have, over open trays is that there is less likely to be damage to the new roots when potting on.

Cutting off the shoot

Preparing the cutting

Clean cut below leaf joint

One major action to take with the cutting is to ensure that it is firmly bedded in the rooting medium. This can be done using a dibber and watered in.

If full-size or half trays are used, the cuttings should be 4 cm apart. Some growers have made a multi-dibber the size to fit the tray and holes are made by pressing the multi-dibber into the rooting compost. Always water in newly placed cuttings to leave no gaps around the base of the stem.

The best results will be obtained if the cuttings can be sprayed with moisture two or three times per day. Some raisers install automatic misting if they cannot be there during the day. In any case, cuttings should be shaded from direct sunlight for the first two weeks. Cuttings raised in the home on a window sill should be out of direct sunlight on a north-facing window. Dahlias will not root if placed in a glass with water, as fuchsias can.

The second method of taking cuttings that can be used is when leaf cuttings are taken. Each leaf has a tiny axial bud growing between the leaf and the main stem of the plant. Left alone, these tiny axial buds will be the branches of the mature plant.

Leaf cuttings are taken when the tiny axial bud is detached with a sliver of the main stem together with its leaf bud. Then the same procedure is adopted as for "normal" cuttings. However this time even more attention will be required to ensure the leaf cutting is firmly fixed in the rooting compost.

Cuttings ready to insert
into rooting medium

Making hole in
rooting medium

Cuttings placed in
rooting medium

Rooted cuttings after two weeks, ready for potting up

Cuttings placed in pots

Plants three weeks after potting up

DAHLIA SEEDS

Dahlias are accommodating in that left to maturity, the blooms will end up producing seed heads. As before there are two methods for producing seeds.

The first is just to let nature take its course, that is let bees and insects pollinate the blooms and take what nature provides. The second method is to try to impose your will on nature by hand pollinating the bloom.

For hand pollinating,, remove the outer petals and expose the stamen, then most hybridists use a brush or piece of fur to transfer pollen to the stigma. Try to accomplish this around midday as the pollen reacts better around then. Whichever method is used, the outcome is not necessarily perfect.

The resulting seed heads should be left as long as possible on the plant, thereby preventing further flowering on that stem and sending a message to the plant of "job done".

Seed pods dried ready for extraction of seed.

Each seed head can provide a dozen or more seeds. Break open the seed heads and dry the seeds and place in a packet with the name attached and place

Seed pod broken open showing seed amongst husks

Husk and seed ready for winnowing

Husk blown away leaving seed

Seed ready for packeting.

in the salad drawer of your kitchen fridge, this will ensure that they stay dry over the winter.

The seed can be sown as for any bedding plant in moist compost and within ten days they will appear and grow on as an independent plant and then they can be given the same treatment as rooted cuttings.

Whatever parents are used, there is no guarantee that the next generation of dahlia will take after either parent. As dahlias are hybrids, each seedling is a potential new cultivar. New seedling plants are usually planted about 20 cm apart, in a custom-made seed bed. The seed bed will be very colourful, containing a large proportion of single blooms, mixed with some double blooms.

Some hybridists find that after planting and growing 1,000 new plants, perhaps about six are worth growing again a second year and after growing a second time perhaps two are worth growing again.

This is because not many seedlings are better than existing cultivars, but hybridising can be exciting in so far as the ones you produce could be not only unique but turn out to be champions, carrying the name you have given them.

POTTING ON

This takes place during the growing season in April and May, before planting out.

Dahlia plants are at their best when there is even growth throughout this period, try to avoid plants growing irregularly or "leggy" between leaf joints. Give them plenty of light and do not keep them too warm.

Ideally, for most of their life dahlia plants need to be "lush", that is soft, whilst the stem is firm enough to sustain growth structure without too much artificial support.

After the final potting on, into 11 cm diameter pots, consideration should be given to "hardening off" the plants before planting out. Ideally, the young plants should be placed in a cold frame from which late spring frosts can be excluded.

PLANTING OUT

Dahlias at whatever stage of their existence succumb to frosts. It makes sense therefore, not to plant out before frosts are finished in your area. That time, as more experienced local gardeners will tell you, is when the soil has warmed and the weather looks set fair.

The alternative, but probably labour intensive, is after planting out early to then provide frost protection. For example, pompons for exhibition are often best produced on second flush, that is after first blooms have been cut, so early plants are needed that are ready to plant out earlier than the other cultivars. These early young plants can be protected if large clay pots or horticultural fleece, newspaper or similar are placed over the plants at night.

The hole dug ready

If your plants have been grown in a compost which contains little or no soil, it helps the plant to get established if the rooting medium in their pot is fairly moist prior to planting.

A hole is dug with a trowel or similar device, wide enough and deep enough to accommodate the plant's roots and its rooting medium.

The hole should be deep enough to allow a slight depression around the plant after planting, which is initially to retain water for the plant if watering becomes necessary and to "puddle in" the newly installed plant.

Unless high temperatures occur or there are drought conditions, the newly planted out plants should be left for about ten days to settle into their new surroundings and then become acclimatised before further watering.

WATERING

After this settling in period a systematic watering regime should be considered, as dahlias will not succeed without sufficient water.

The pot removed, showing
a vigorous root system

The plant placed in the hole

Firming in, leaving
a depression

If you have decided on attempting to exhibit, watering must be seriously considered and undertaken.

This may be done by hand, watering by hose or can or by drip lines using perforated hose which can be hand or automatically operated.

During the blooming season in summer and early autumn about a gallon per day per plant is ideal if growing for exhibition.

STOPPING

Left to its own devices the dahlia will produce one very strong central stem and a large but probably coarse single flower. This is because the hormone auxin is produced in the central stem which suppresses side growths.

When the plant is well established the growing centre of the plant should be removed, preferably near the top pair of leaves, again usually by thumb and first finger or by a sharp blade. This is removing the growing centre or "stopping". It has the effect on the plant of reducing or removing the production of auxin and thus allows equally strong side branches

The growing tip, highlighted

Preparing to snap
the growing tip

The tip breaking off

The tip removed

to be produced. It also affects the timing of the first blooms. If you are just growing for garden pleasure then stopping as early as possible is a good idea.

Growing to get blooms on or near a specific date for exhibition requires knowing the cultivar and climatic conditions for your area, and an educated guess as to the likely climatic conditions for the coming growing season. Talk to an exhibitor who will always give advice on individual cultivar stopping times for your area.

A lot is written and talked about of the science of "stopping", however it has to be understood that the dahlia is a "lush" plant which responds to hot and humid weather such that the life of a bloom may only be 24 hours instead of several days.

Only experience will fully help in selecting your stopping date, plus the knowledge that most giant cultivars require an earlier date than other types.

Each lateral branch will in due time produce a bloom, and each lateral branch will have lateral buds which in turn produce lateral branches.

Left alone after stopping, a large bush will be produced with lots of blooms, excellent for the garden but not for producing exhibition blooms.

DISBUDDING AND TIMING YOUR BLOOMS

Dahlia blooms need a certain amount of time to develop after the first pea sized bud is seen at the end of your chosen stem. If you remember, we have by now limited the amount of stems on your plants for exhibiting to four stems on large and giant cultivars, six stems on medium cultivars and perhaps eight on small cultivars and so on.

Buds appearing at the growing tip of shoot

Top two side buds removed

When the terminal bud appears, it needs to be secured. That is, the side buds below it down the stem need to be removed by snapping them off with the thumb and forefingers. For smalls, you can remove the growths down two pairs of leaves, for mediums three pairs and for large and giant maybe down four pairs of leaves or even more. Try to spread the disbudding per stem over perhaps three or four days.

Once the buds are secured this way they will develop into flowers in about three to four weeks. The time at which they flower can be affected by unusu-

ally warm or cold conditions making them flower early or late respectively, but as a general guide allow 28 days for large and giant cultivars, down to 20 days for small cultivars. So by looking at your show date, say on the August Bank Holiday, which is around the 28th August, count back the days and you can see that you need to see buds in the giants at the end of July.

I would suggest that if any buds appear that would be too early then you could cut back those stems down to the third set of leaves and let one side shoot develop on this stem. Doing this will provide some flowers for the later shows as they would otherwise be wasted if they bloom too early.

Timing is not an important factor when growing for garden flowers, but some light disbudding will improve the quality of the blooms as they appear in your garden, as it will give larger flowers with better colour and strong stems.

TYPES

Earlier in the book it was suggested that you work to a plan and decide on what to grow. It has been emphasised that dahlias come in all sorts of shapes and sizes as well as colours.

The National Dahlia Society produces, every other year, a Classified Directory for sale. This details the different types of dahlias as well as sizes and recommendations for the use of the various varieties. In addition, it incorporates the rules for judging dahlias. Types covered include single, anemone, collerette, waterlily, decorative, ball, pompon, cactus, semi-cactus and miscellaneous as well as fimbriated, double orchid, single orchid and paeony. Also included are border, patio and gallery dahlias, lilliput dahlias and bedding dahlias.

The criteria for classifying dahlias is by examining individual petal formations of a bloom that occur about two thirds of the way back in a full bloom. It depends on degree and direction of curl on the longitudinal axis of the petal whether the variety is classified as cactus, semi cactus, decorative, waterlily, ball or pom. Size is also catered for in the Classified Directory and is based on International Dahlia Standards. (Judging Rules allow a margin above this size before disqualification is invoked but with a margin that allows for exhibition purposes. Blooms in excess of the following sizes will be disqualified: pompon 52 mm, miniature 115 mm, small 170 mm, medium 220 mm, large 260 mm.)

In the Classification Grouping, size, colour and use for each listed cultivar is provided. The usages are G for Garden, C for Cut Flower E for Exhibition and P for Pot or Patio use. The alphabetical list provided gives the classification group for each cultivar listed, the raiser, the country of origin and the year of raising (where known).

Avoca Amanda, a medium
decorative type

Kilmorie, a small semi-cactus

Wishes and Dreams, a single
dahlia with dark foliage

Scarlett Claire,
a collerette dahlia

Lauren Kitchener,
a multi-layer collerette

A fimbriated dahlia

A pom dahlia with blooms around 50mm diameter

It should be noted that if a variety is classified in the directory, it can only be exhibited in the defined category. There is therefore a wealth of information contained in the directory to help your decision on what to grow.

EXHIBITING DAHLIAS

The first question to be asked is how much time do you have available to tend the dahlias? One hour per day per hundred is necessary from about a month after planting out, until the show season is over; not six hours on Sunday and nothing during the week!

The second question to ask yourself is: will you protect your exhibition blooms from wind and rain, if so how? Nothing can be more soul destroying for an exhibitor than to having spent time and money to produce exhibition-standard dahlia blooms, on time for a show, to have the blooms damaged by weather.

A number of protective options are available, including over-all plastic, individual umbrellas or cones made from semi rigid wire covered with plastic. It is fair to say that none of these methods are perfect but use of any or a mixture can help to preserve the blooms against weather damage.

Whichever method is used, it is vital that the fixing both of the protection and the blooms is firm and secure. Otherwise the risk is that the blooms will be damaged by rubbing against the protection.

The worse case scenario is that gale force winds would send the protective umbrella sailing across the dahlia patch causing mayhem to many plants. The height of the protection provided can also be critical, if the cultivar grows to two metres or more, there must be headroom clearance.

The protection must also be capable of handling an overnight or day-long downpour of rain. It is quite amazing how much water can accumulate on flat plastic surfaces even when slanted quite steeply.

Winning at anything often requires being ruthless and the dahlia world is no exception. Genuine winners, however, can accept losing graciously in the knowledge that, usually, what goes around comes around.

- Be ruthless! You may have bought a 'world beater' which turns out to be anything but. So, unless you have good reason, discard it – unless you want a second season of disappointment.
- Similarly, your special favourite may become diseased, in which case burn it and get new stock.
- Grow not necessarily what you like, but what wins.
- Look at show results, remembering however that some growers can coax winning blooms from cultivars that no one else can.
- Always mark each season, the plants that have done well for you, producing winning blooms and propagate only from those tubers for next year's plants.

Having successfully produced exhibition blooms to your satisfaction, carefully cutting them is the first successful step in exhibiting. Never cut blooms in full sunlight. The best time for cutting dahlia blooms is either early morning or early evening. If the day is overcast or not too hot it is possible to cut blooms without causing blooms to wilt.

For giants, it is a must – and with mediums equally essential – to cane the stem of the selected bloom usually some days prior to cutting by fixing an appropriately-sized split cane to the stem with two or more twistit ties.

Dahlias appreciate standing in water for a period before travelling. Preferably this should be done in a dark, dry and cool place, usually a garage.

Cutting should always be done with a sharp knife, slanting at a forty five degree angle across the stem, to maximise stem wall contact with the water.

Many giants and some other cultivars with large hollow stems appreciate being pierced below the water line to release air from the stem, if this is not done the bloom may not take up water and its back petals collapse. This could be done using something like a knitting needle or your knife, turning it slightly to open the hole up. Ensure, however, that the piercing is not above the water line or the bloom will collapse.

Next in importance is protecting the blooms from damage in transit. A hundred years ago blooms were transported to shows dry, on soft tissues in florist's boxes. That still works, particularly if after taking the stem from the water it is plugged to retain the water in the stem. Using this system, further time is required as the blooms need to go into water at the show before staging.

However, nowadays dahlias are transported to shows either in drums filled with water or on hurdles with water containers fixed to the bottom of the hurdle. It is essential that during travel there is no movement of the blooms.

With the drums, holes are drilled around the rim so that the caned stems can be fixed with "Twistits" and chicken wire place in the bottom of the drum. Alternatively, the drum can contain foam rubber or plastic to hold the stems in position.

Hurdles usually have plastic tubes for water fixed to the bottom rail and two further rails to fix the stems to with Twistits.

Always check on drumming up or fixing to the hurdles that the height of the cut blooms easily clears the vehicle head room. It's useful to have a cane cut to size beforehand, as a measure for cutting heights clearing the headroom.

Blooms caned and fastened in drums for transport to show

Blooms fastened in specially made hurdles to fit in the car

BE PREPARED

Read the show schedule, before setting out to the show. You have planted enough plants to ensure sufficient blooms will be produced so, before setting out, check that you have cut enough blooms as the schedule may have changed. So ensure you have enough cut enough blooms to stage what you have entered.

Many a disaster has occurred because of being one bloom short of requirements when staging. It is useful to have substitutes with you, as occasionally disaster strikes whilst exhibitors are staging..

Arrive at the show venue in good time. Ensure that you have all the accoutrements: knife, scissors, oasis, cotton buds, tweezers pens, etc. You would be surprised how many times exhibitors forget essentials.

Are the vases provided, or do you have to provide your own?

It may sound daft, but exhibitors (and judges) have been known to arrive a day early or a day late, or an hour or so late, even a week late or at the wrong venue!

Assuming that you arrive at the right venue in good time, particularly at a new venue, before you do anything, walk around the show and staging areas and get the feel of the place before unloading your blooms.

Look for potential hazards: the wet leaf on the floor, the mini step where you least expect it. You will not want to have spent time and money getting good blooms to the show venue only to have disaster strike.

Blooms should be staged so that the stems are fixed firmly in the vase as the judges will pick up your vase from the bench to properly examine the blooms from all angles. Oasis is the medium mostly used in the vase nowadays for this purpose, but newspaper cut or torn into quarters and rolled into balls can be a good substitute, particularly with giant varieties.

Bullrushes or similar multi-tissue plant stems can also be used, but make sure, however, that no herbicide has been used in their vicinity.

Make up a number of vases with your staging medium, say four or five. Fill these up with water – blooms without water in their vase will quickly go soft at the back.

Are three or five blooms required? There is no rule on whether to stage one in a back row or two, nor whether there should be two or thee blooms in the back row. Select the height for blooms in the front and back rows and spacing between blooms that will show off the blooms to their best advantage

First impressions may help with a well-staged set of blooms.

Blooms should sit on their stems desirably either at forty five degrees, (except pompons), or sitting fully on top. Even with the best of growing, it may not be possible to match each bloom required for this situation. With two blooms at forty five degrees to the stem and one sitting on top of the stem it may well be that instead of one in the back row the best result can be achieved with two in the back row.

In multi-vase classes, the vases should all match, that is similar numbers in back and front rows for each vase and be at the same height.

It has to be recorded that many good results are achieved mixing cultivars in a vase, if they match for size and degree of angle, when competing with a vase containing all of the same cultivar.

Having decided on which blooms to use, first use an NDS approved judging ring, of the appropriate size, to ensure the blooms are not oversize.

It takes time to stage a vase of blooms and it is very annoying to be disqualified, particularly for one oversize bloom in an exhibit of, say, five vases. The oversize may well be because of one or two petals sticking out. If so, carefully remove it or them with a pair of tweezers.

If the tips of the petals touch the inside of the rings the vase should be disqualified. So do not take a chance – if you have replacement blooms, use them.

A superbly staged exhibit of small cactus/semi-cactus cultivars

A bad way out, if there are too many petals to pull out or if you do not have replacements, is to snip the end of the culprit petals. This can only be a last-minute action, as any average judge will spot and seriously down point your entry as containing damage to the bloom. Not to be recommended.

Having chosen the blooms to use, do not be in too much of a hurry to cut the stem of the bloom. Try the selected blooms in different combinations in the vase including height, until you are satisfied.

Remove carefully with tweezers any damaged petals as what the judge does not see, he or she cannot down-point.

Be careful, however – damage to the front of the blooms is a serious fault. If necessary, clean off any small deficiencies with a cotton bud. Cotton buds can also be used to roll back petals that are not layering properly.

At last the vase is to your satisfaction; check it for water and top up as necessary.

In multi-vase classes, each vase should join the other vases in making an exhibit where all heights of staged vases combine to produce a harmonious composition overall.

Make sure that all of your blooms are named; also that you place your entry in the space allocated to the class. Remember: although judges and show officials are at the show to get the best results for the show, they also can make mistakes. An easy one missed is if, for example, a larger number of entries occurs for the class and your entry ends up on a space not obviously part of the class.

If you finish staging with time to spare, which should be your aim, go around the hall and check your exhibits. This is where prizes are won or lost. You must be critical of your exhibit and what the competition has staged. Will that vase you have staged compete with the competition? Have you a better vase? Have you time to change the exhibit? Those final few moments can be the test of the exhibitor's skill.

Whatever the outcome, accept that judge's verdict – unless for you the decision is glaringly wrong, in which case follow the complaint procedure in the schedule.

What you will find is friendship and a great camaraderie, combined with great rivalry in the exhibition world.

CALENDAR OF ACTIVITIES

Where does the Dahlia year begin? A good place to start is when the plants are blackened by frost.

EARLY WINTER:
LATE NOVEMBER & DECEMBER

Frosts will have blackened the dahlia plants. With the remains of the plants cut down to ground level, the crown of the tubers now needs protection. Do you dig them out and store or do you leave them in?

If not dug up but left in the ground, the crown and tubers require at least an inch of insulating medium against frost, peat or straw, as a covering, together with anti slug measures. If dug up, the tubers and crown will require attention. Remove damaged tubers or any areas of fungal attack. Treat with fungicide and store them in a frost proof, dry place. They can be buried in the soil of the borders of the greenhouse.

Roughly dig the area of soil for next year's planting. Sterilise the soil if disease has occurred during the growing season.

Study traders' catalogues. Order new ones as necessary.

MID-WINTER:
DURING JANUARY & FEBRUARY

Move the tubers from their storage. Check again for mildew or rot and treat as necessary. Set the tubers up in a heated greenhouse or on a heated bench. A desirable greenhouse minimum night temperature of 10 degrees centigrade is necessary.

The tubers can be placed directly in a bed of compost on the bench or in suitable trays. The latter is helpful when taking cuttings because the tray can be moved for ease of reach for taking cuttings.

Watch out for slugs and snails awaking from hibernation and destroy.

Start the tubers off with warm or hot water then water at greenhouse temperature. Compost must not be overwatered.

Towards the end of this period, lightly fork over or hoe the growing area.

EARLY SPRING: MARCH & APRIL

With the right treatment the tubers will have sprouted many shoots. Carefully take cuttings below the first pair of leaves ensuring little or no damage to the crown. Do not be greedy as taking too many cuttings can lead to weakened plants and weakened plants are ready victims of diseases.

Have a system of labelling such that each cutting is easily identified throughout its life cycle.

Spray cuttings as often as possible, morning and evening, and keep them from full sunlight. Cuttings prosper in humid conditions. Pot on rooted cuttings as soon as possible.

Take early delivery of new stock of plants and climatise these.

Maintain throughout a spraying regime against pests and diseases.

Towards the end of this period, "harden off" all plants in frost-proof frames.

Check plot watering arrangements and hoe off any weeds.

LATE SPRING: MAY & JUNE

Spread and hoe in inorganic fertilizers at recommended rates to the soil of the plot. Then lay out any mulching material, marking out planting places. Provide support canes at recommended distances.

Plant out the hardened off plants or divided field tubers when the danger of frost no longer exists.

Fix first plant supports. Then relax.

SUMMER: JULY & AUGUST

After plants have adjusted to planting out, take out the growing centre (stop). It is useful for each variety to stop a proportion at intervals. This can ensure a continuation of blooms over a period during the flowering season.

Keep down weeds. Ensure regular watering. (90% of the dahlia is water). Continue the spraying regime.

If using straw, manure or similar mulch, spread carefully between plants avoiding stem contact.

Liquid feed using a nitrogen feed as necessary.

Destroy any virused plants.

A week before showing blooms, introduce covering against wind and rain and also consider shading some giant types against sun damage.

Check bloom transport system. Also plant supports, provide additional supports if necessary.

EARLY AUTUMN: SEPTEMBER

Cut and enjoy exhibition blooms. Enter shows.

Mark those plants providing best blooms for next year's parent plants.

Change the liquid feed to higher potash.

Continue spraying against pests and diseases.

Take off side shoots according to variety, to maintain good quality blooms.

LATE AUTUMN: OCTOBER & EARLY NOVEMBER

Thoroughly clean any greenhouse or area used for propagation. Similarly remove canes or stakes used for supporting plants, clean and disinfect before winter storage.

Order propagation and other next year's items.

If early frost, start digging.

PESTS

Like most great hobbies in life, yes, dahlia growing is, after all, only a hobby. There are enemies of the dahlia. Do not be put off by the following list of pests and diseases: with culture and good husbandry most can be avoided or overcome.

EARWIGS

There are many myths about the earwig. There are several varieties of earwig but they all are insects with slender, many-jointed antennae and a pair of appendages resembling forceps. With these the earwigs can render a bloom useless in no time at all, as well as destroying foliage.

Bloom showing earwig damage and still containing the earwig

The earwig is mostly nocturnal but sometimes likes to forage at times during the day.

The best method for dealing with earwigs is prevention rather than cure.

Earwigs tend to mate during winter and survive in garden debris, old leaves or in cracks and crevices in trees and wooden fences. All the earwigs on your dahlia patch will have been there over winter.

Hunt them out before you have the supply of food they need and like, your mature dahlia plants and blooms.

Kill them with paraffin or hot water, being careful not to splash plant foliage, or squash them between thumb and forefinger, or beneath your boot. Do not plug bamboo cane supports; use these as traps down which to drip paraffin.

Traps can also be set using straw in pots on the top of canes, placed at strategic points in the garden. Tip your captures into paraffin or hot water.

RED SPIDER

These, of course, are not actually red spiders but microscopic spider mites that, although individually brown, appear en-masse to be red.

The affect of infestation by these mites on a plant is to cause loss of vigour, meaning also damage to or distortion of blooms as well as with bad infestation the loss of the plant. To avoid any of this happening, regularly spray with a proprietary insecticide on both sides of the leaves. Also just spraying with water both sides of leaves can reduce the possibility of infestation as they live mostly on the undersides.

The life cycle of a red spider mite is ten days. That is, if adults are killed any eggs laid will hatch out in ten days. So if you discover this pest it is necessary to spray at ten-day intervals.

The red spider thrives in a hot, dry climate so a water spray will help. Just like the earwig, the red spider hibernates over winter in the trees, bushes, wooden fences and posts in or around your dahlia plot.

A spray during early spring or late winter with the appropriate insecticide of these surfaces will help reduce if not eliminate this pest. They will also over-winter on your tubers, so spray again when setting your tubers up for propagation.

OTHER INSECTS

Thrips, black fly, green fly and white fly will inevitably attack your dahlias, in the greenhouse particularly, and given the right climatic conditions, during the outdoor growing season. These are easily dealt with by setting up a programme of regular spraying with insecticide.

CATERPILLARS

An eaten bloom showing caterpillar

Much like slugs and snails, they will damage your blooms and plants. A difficult decision here if you like butterflies and moths, but be ruthless and use your insecticide carefully. Or pick off and keep in an appropriate jar with leaves supplied until they mature.

SLUGS AND SNAILS

These molluscs also enjoy the fruits of your labours; particularly the growing eyes on the crown of the tuber, the nearly perfect show bloom and just about any part of the dahlia plant that they can get their rasping under-belly to reach.

Kill using pellets of Metaldehyde, or a liquid version on the soil, remembering that some pellets are harmful to birds and pets, so use carefully.

WASPS

Wasps like the sugar content of the dahlia stems. If wasps are plentiful they will cause problems by removing sections from stems. Be particularly careful when disbudding as they seem to disappear into the foliage.

As pests they vary from year to year but once they find dahlia plots they like, they seem to remember and come back. Spray again with insecticide to discourage as they seem immune to most sprays, otherwise find the nest and liberally dose it with Jeyes Fluid.

OTHER PESTS (FOUR-LEGGED)

Rural growers will know that there are enemies of dahlias with four legs: rabbits, deer and cows to mention some.

Fencing of the plot is a necessity and the only solution. In the case of rabbits or deer, mesh of sufficient height and with a good six inches of it buried in the ground. With cows a solid fence is necessary and don't forget to close any gates.

DISEASES

VIRUS

The most deadly disease of the dahlia is virus. This comes in many different disguises. Cucumber mosaic and dahlia mosaic to name but two versions. The signs of all viruses are a mottling of the leaves or veining and dwarfing of the plants. The distance between joints of the plant appear shorter than normal. It is a very serious condition.

Two plants of the same cultivar showing virus on the front plant, whilst the rear plant is growing normally

Regrettably, healthy-looking plants can quickly deteriorate and become infected. There are some varieties that whilst immune from the effects of virus, are carriers of the disease, for example some plants of the Bishop of Llandaff are suspect.

Currently there is no cure. The American Dahlia Society has commissioned research for a cure but after ten tears has found no cure. There are also indications from the US research that virus can be transmitted in pollen when hybridising, so try to avoid using the pollen from affected plants.

Pull up and burn any suspect plant, whatever it cost you to purchase or how much you may cherish its blooms.

The virus is spread by sap-sucking insects which move from plant to plant in your dahlia plot and from your neighbours plot, thereby spreading the virus if it is around.

Also, the use of the blade to take cuttings will spread virus if you are unfortunate enough to have an infected tuber. Try to sterilise your blade, with Jeyes Fluid or any strong disinfectant, between taking cuttings from tubers. Some growers keep separate razor blades for each tuber!

CROWN GALL

Crown galls are growths that appear on the crown of the tuber, looking a bit like miniature cauliflowers. They are caused by damage to the plant tissue allowing bacteria from the soil to enter the plant.

If the plant is of value to you, remove these growths and take cuttings from elsewhere on the crown; otherwise discard the tubers. Do not take cuttings from the gall area.

FUNGAL INFECTION

Humid growing conditions give rise to fungal infection of dahlias. Smut is the most prevalent. This starts with yellow or brown rings on lower leaves which quickly spread to higher leaves. Fungal spores from the ground travel up onto leaves during rain or watering.

Powdery mildew showing on the leaves

Remove all dead leaves and affected leaves as soon as possible. Spray with a proprietary fungicide and treat soil of the plot also with a fungicide. Using fabric mulch will reduce this problem.

Mildew has become a minor problem recently and is blown in from surrounding gardens. It is not helped if there is dryness at the roots of the plants. Regular spraying with a fungicide is nessary once spotted on your plot.

PROTECTING TUBERS

The crown of the roots (tubers) does not survive really hard frosts. Since the crown is located about an inch or so below the soil surface it has, in the UK, to be a really hard penetrating frost to harm the crown.

In most years this does not happen; what does happen is that, during early spring, slugs start to become active. What better feast for a slug than the new eyes of your dahlia tubers, excellent for the early slug's breakfast or dinner? You will not see them below ground so in spring, if you have not lifted your tubers, fork in some slug pellets.

If growing for garden use it is probably enough to cover the old tubers with a 3 cm or so of peat, straw or leaf mould until frosts are gone and new shoots are showing.

Dahlias for exhibition can be a different matter altogether. Exhibition growers usually lift their dahlias after or near to the first winter frost, when the plants have turned black.

Cut down to ground level the old dead plant material, which should be disposed of in such a way that it will not give you trouble next year, i.e. burnt or despatched to the local authority waste disposal site. Tubers should be carefully lifted with a fork to minimise damage to the tubers. Any seriously damaged ones should be cut off. Examine the tubers, crown and any portion of old main stem for signs of fungus and treat with sulphur powder anyway. Only about one inch of main stem above the crown should be left so cut off the rest. If the stem is hollow, cut out the centre and, if need be, cut the crown and stem in two to remove any plant material that might rot. With a very wet period before lifting there is a case for leaving the tubers upside

Pot tubers growing, buried up to the rim of the pot

down on the green house or shed bench to drain so that any residual water retained in the crown of main stem is released.

What will you do with the tubers for a couple of months or so? Firstly, frost-proof storage is a necessity. If that cannot be a greenhouse, shed, garage or house, then consider a clamp somewhere in the garden or dahlia plot, protected from wind and pests as far as possible, or bury them in your greenhouse border.

During the last world war, many farmers clamped root vegetables and dahlia tubers are not much different. A clamp can be provided by a three or four inch layer of straw, then a layer of tubers, followed by another layer of straw and so on until a final layer of straw on top of which is a rainproof cover, firmly fastened down to prevent wind disturbance. Each layer of straw should contain some slug pellets. Remember: first in, last out, so late-flowering varieties requiring early plants would go in last.

There is an alternative to above-ground clamps. A hole can be dug in the garden and the process just described repeated, provided your neighbours do not think the hole is for your partner! Normally,

71

Tuber, having just been dug, is labelled securely

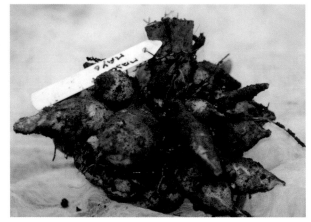

The tuber cleaned and trimmed for storage

however, after storage the tubers are set up on a heated bed, either directly on a bed of compost on the bench, or in trays or boxes of compost. The tubers are hardy so a dip in very hot water with a mild disinfectant is a good way to wake them from their winter slumbers. In about fourteen days, shoots will appear and the cycle of cutting, potting on, feeding, spraying and planting out can begin.

Pot tubers are a very sure way of keeping the stock of a particular cultivar that you may not want to lose. The way to deal with these is to have maybe two or three extra plants in the pots you use prior to planting out and to bury these in the ground up to the neck of the pot. The pots are not removed and the plants can be treated as you would the main plants except that, once you have established that the flower is the one on the label, the plant is then not allowed to produce any further flowers. All top growth is cut down each time buds appear.

In this way the strength of the cultivar is concentrated in a small, confined tuber which is easy to store after lifting. Also, invariably, these small tubers are very vigorous when started into growth on your greenhouse bench.

Pot tubers lifted and stored over winter in their pots

MODERN EXHIBITION DAHLIAS

What are you going to grow? The choice is yours and there are plenty to choose from.

Already in this book it has been recommended that you plan what to do and stick to it, in terms of total numbers to grow and guidance on how to break that total into numbers to grow, of any one type or variety.

An arrangement of dahlia *Lilyanna W*, a lilliput dahlia

What cannot be recommended are the numbers or types to grow; only you can do that. One person's delight, be it collerettes or pompon, cactus or decorative is another person's bad dream.

What follows are brief descriptions of the possibilities and use of the National Dahlia Society Classified Directory and Judging Rules will help here.

POMPON DAHLIAS

For exhibition, pompon dahlias should be perfectly globular. They should have fully double spherical blooms of miniature size (maximum size 50 mm in diameter) with florets largely involute along their longitudinal axis. For exhibition purposes blooms should face upwards on a firm, straight stem.

Gurtla Twilight	UK, raised 1996, white with pink blends.
Hallmark	Australian, raised 1960, pink with lavender blends
Moor Place	UK, raised 1957, purple
Noreen	Australia, raised 1962, pink & purple blends
Rhonda	Australia, raised in 1947, lavender and white blends
Will's Ringwood Rosie	UK, raised 2004, red
Willo's Violet	Australian, raised 1937, purple blends

The fact that most of these varieties were raised so long ago is a tribute to how good they are and that they are still grown and winning most prizes.

There are many more good varieties of pompons available, but those above are the best.

DECORATIVES

For exhibition, decoratives (and cactus, and semi-cactus blooms) should be fresh and clean. Florets should be intact, firm and without blemish or defect.

The colour should be clear and well defined and either consistent or evenly shaded or tipped throughout the bloom. Blooms should be poised at an angle not less than 45 degrees to the stem.

They should have fully double blooms showing no disc. The ray florets are either flat, partially involute, partially revolute or slightly twisted, the tip is bluntly pointed or indented.

A giant decorative flower shown with the 260 mm ring

Giant decoratives have blooms exceeding 250 mm in diameter:

Alva's Supreme	New Zealand, raised 1956, yellow
Bryn Terfel	New Zealand, raised 2004, red
Jean Shaw	UK, raised 2009, bronze and orange blends

Kidd's Climax	New Zealand, raised 1940, pink & yellow blends
Sir Alf Ramsey	UK, raised 1999, lavender and white blends
White Alva's Supreme	UK, raised 1979, white.

Large decorative blooms between 200 mm and 250 mm in diameter:

Elma E	USA, raised 1993, lavender
Grace Kendall	UK, raised 2003, yellow
Kenora Wildfire	USA, raised 1990, red
Ryecroft Ice	UK, raised 2009, white
Silver City	UK, raised 1967, white
Spartacus	USA, raised 1992, red
Willowfield Mick	UK, raised 1999, orange pink blends

Medium decorative blooms between 150 mm and 200 mm in diameter:

Andrea Clark	UK, raised 1999, yellow
Alf's Mascot	UK, raised 2001, white
Avoca Amanda	UK, raised 2008, pink
B.J.Beauty	UK, raised 1976, white
Charlie Two	UK, raised 1989, yellow
Trengrove Millenium	UK, raised 2000, yellow

A small decorative dahlia

Small decorative blooms between 100 mm and
150 mm in diameter:

Ryecroft Brenda T   UK, raised 20078, white

Gateshead Festival   UK, raised 1990
                         orange pink blends

Marion Storer   UK, raised 2008, red

Ruby   UK, raised 2008, red

Ruskin Diane   UK, raised 1984, yellow

Winholme Diane   UK, raised 2000, yellow

Miniature decorative blooms not exceeding
100 mm in diameter:

Barbarry Pip   UK, raised 2006, red

Blyton Lady in Red   UK, raised 2005, red

Marston Lilac   UK, raised 2003, lilac

Rosendale Lewis   UK, raised 2009, yellow

Ryecroft Jan   UK, raised 2001, white

WATERLILY FLOWER

Have fully double blooms characterised by broad and generally sparse ray florets, which are straight or slightly involute along their length giving the flower a shallow appearance. The depth should be less than half the diameter of the bloom.

Giant, large & medium flower:

None

Small flower between 100 mm and 150 mm in diameter:

Bracken Ballerina	Australia, raised 1988, pink
Cameo	Australia, raised 1986, yellow
Charlie Dimmock	UK, raised 2005, orange
Sheps Memory	UK, raised 2006, yellow red blends
Taratahi Ruby	New Zealand, raised 1999, red

Miniature flower not exceeding 100 mm in diameter:

None

Claire Louise Kitchener, a pink waterlily

BALL DAHLIAS

Have fully
double blooms
showing no
disc, ball
shaped
or slightly flat-
tened. Their
ray florets are
displayed in
a spiral
arrangement
and are
involute and
round at the
tip. Blooms must be poised at an angle of not less than
45 degrees to the stem.

Small ball dahlias between 100 mm and 150 mm
in diameter:

Amy Cave	UK, raised 2007, purple
Blyton Softer Gleam	UK raised 2005, yellow & orange blends
Charlie Briggs	UK, raised 2001, orange
Cherwell Linnet	UK, raised 2006, orange

Miniature Ball not exceeding 100 mm in diameter:

Hamari Rose	UK, raised 1993, pink
Jomanda	Holland, raised 1996, orange
L'Ancresse	UK, raised 1982, white
Mary's Jomanda	UK, raised 2002, purple
Ryecroft Laura	UK, raised 2008, yellow

SEMI-CACTUS DAHLIAS

Should have fully double blooms, the ray florets are usually pointed and revolute for more than 25% and less than 50% of their length and broad at the base and either straight or incurving.

Giant flower exceeding 250 mm:

Janal Amy   UK, raised 1999, yellow

Rose Jupiter   UK, raised 1986, pink

A yellow giant semi-cactus dahlia, *Janal Amy*

Large flower between 200 mm and 250 mm in diameter:

Hamari Accord   UK, raised 1986, yellow

Hamari Katrina   UK, raised 1972, yellow

Kenora Challenger   USA, raised 1991, white

Kenora Jubilee   USA, raised 2001, white

Salmon Keene   UK, raised 1978, pink blends

Medium flower between 150 mm and 200 mm in diameter:

Coxwell Moonlight	UK, raised 2000, yellow
Cream Moonlight	UK, raised 2001, yellow
Grenidor Pastelle	UK, raised 1988, pink yellow blends
Peach Delight	Australia, raised 2004, pink blends
Ruskin Michelle	UK, raised 2006, pink
Ruskin Sunshine	UK, raised 2003, yellow
White Moonlight	UK, raised 1984, white

Small flower between 100 mm and 150 mm in diameter:

Cherwell Goldcrest	UK, raised 1996, yellow blends
Jackie Magson	UK, raised 1996, orange
Kilmorie	UK raised 2002, pink & yellow blends
Oakwood Goldcrest	UK, raised 2006, yellow
Ruskin Myra	UK, raised 2001, orange yellow blends
Ruskin Respectable	UK raised 2009, orange yellow blends

Miniature flower not exceeding 100 mm in diameter:

Weston Miss	UK raised 2001, yellow
Weston Tea Time	UK raised 2006, yellow pink blends

CACTUS DAHLIAS

Have fully double blooms, the ray florets are usually pointed, the majority narrow and revolute for 50% or more of their length (longitudinal axis) and either straight or incurving.

Giant flower over 250 mm in diameter:

None

Large flower between 200 mm and 250 mm in diameter:

None

Medium flower between 150 mm and 200 mm in diameter:

Classic Al	USA, raised 1994, yellow
Raiser's Pride	Holland, raised 1960, pink & yellow blends

Small flower between 100 mm and 150 mm in diameter:

Deborah's Kiwi	UK, raised 1996, pink & white blends
Kiwi Gloria	UK, raised 1998, lavender blends
Lavender Athalie	UK, raised 1981, lavender
Trelyn Kiwi	UK raised 1996, white & pink blends

Trelyn Kiwi, a small cactus dahlia

Miniature flower not exceeding 100 mm in diameter:

So Dainty   UK, raised 1973,
                       bronze blends

Weston Dove   UK, raised 2001,
                       white & lilac blends

Weston Nugget   UK, raised 1995, bronze

Weston Pirate   UK, raised 1998, red

Weston Spanish   UK, raised 2000,
Dancer   red & yellow blends

COLLERETTE DAHLIAS

Have blooms with a single outer ring of generally flat ray florets which may overlap, with a ring of small florets (the collar) the centre forming a disc.

Ann Breckenfelder   Holland, raised 2004,
red & yellow red blends

Clair de Lune   Holland, raised 1946,
yellow & yellow

Don Hill   UK, raised 2004,
purple & white red blends

Teesbrook Redeye   UK, raised 2005,
lavender & lavender

A collerette dahlia, *Olivia*

85

FIMBRIATED DAHLIAS

Have blooms where ray florets should be evenly split or notched into two or more divisions uniformly throughout the bloom to create a fringed overall effect. The petals may be flat, involute, revolute, straight, incurving or twisted.

Giant flower exceeding 250 mm in diameter:

None

Large flower between 200 mm and 250mm in diameter:

Fidalgo Climax	USA, raised 1991, yellow
Stellyvonne	South Africa, 1989, yellow pink blends

Medium flower between 150 mm and 200 mm in diameter:

Jean Ellen	UK, raised 2010, yellow
Marlene Joy	USA, raised 1989, white pink blends
My Beverley	USA, raised 2001, yellow red blends
Nenekazi	South Africa, raised 1997, bronze pink blends

Small flower between 100 mm and 150 mm in diameter:

None

Polka, an anemone
flowered type

ANEMONE

Anemone flowered dahlias have blooms with one or
more outer rings of generally flattened ray florets
surrounding a dense group of tubular florets and
showing no disc.

Pasodoble   Holland, raised 1993,
                       white and yellow

Ryecroft Marge   UK, raised 2008,
                       yellow and white pink
                       blends

OTHERS

DOUBLE ORCHID

Giraffe, a double orchid dahlia

Have fully double blooms showing no disc, that have triangular shaped centres. Ray florets are narrowly lance shaped and either involute or revolute.

Giraffe   Holland, raised 1948, yellow bronze variegated

Pink Giraffe   UK, raised 1961, pink bronze variegated

SINGLE ORCHID

Have blooms with a single outer ring of florets surrounding a disc. Ray florets are uniformly either involute or revolute.

Honka   USA, raised 1990, yellow

Juul's All Star   USA raised 2001, red & yellow

Marie Schnugg   USA, raised 1973, red

UK PLACES TO VISIT

NDS Exhibition Trials, Golden Acre Park, Leeds

Welsh Dahlia Trials, Pencoed College, Wales

RHS Wisley Gardens, Surrey

Great Dixter Gardens, Sussex

Anglesey Abbey, Cambridge

Bristol Zoo

LIST OF UK TRADERS

Aylett Nurseries, St Albans

Halls of Heddon Nurseries, Northumberland

JRG Dahlias, Milnthorpe, Cumbria

Ridgeway Nursery, West Lothian

Ryecroft Dahlias, Storrington, West Sussex

Station House Nurseries, South Wirral, Cheshire

PICTURE CREDITS

ABOUT THE AUTHOR

Ted Collins, who is presently President of the National Dahlia Society, has accrued many honours from the society over his 40 years as a member.

He has held every senior office since he began serving on the Executive Council and has been awarded both Silver and Gold medals for exceptional service to the dahlia, as well as becoming a Vice President of the NDS.

He is a skilled showman, judge and lecturer and is ably assisted by his wife, Jean, in all his work for the NDS.

Having served as an executive on Slough Council for a number of years, Ted is actively involved with charities training young people for work in the community.

He has travelled the world representing the NDS and this is his fifth book on dahlias.

www.dahlia-nds.co.uk

REG. CHARITY NO. 254049

Jean Ellen (Collins), the
author's wife, with the dahlia
named after her